Reyes's debut collection is the kind of ⌐   ⌐
feel you've landed on the page you need. Reyes is a chronicler of migration
in all its meanings and murmurations and, refreshingly, does not flinch
from her own transgressions. But read front to last, these poems, with
through lines of gender, race, adventure, desire, build into a deeply moving
provocation of loss and discovery.

The brilliance of these poems is their achievement of discomfit as they
simultaneously travel distance and move inward. "This is church" a line
delivers, only to turn in on itself in the next, "this is collateral." The title
of this collection is a promise: how poetry can at once run and stand still,
and why that matters.

VALERIE WALLACE, AUTHOR OF *HOUSE OF MCQUEEN*

In a poem about visiting Kara Walker's "[Marvelous] Sugar Baby," Reyes
writes, "This is church. This is collateral. This is holy terrain. / I am
ekphrasis, imbued to the frame." How powerful is poetry? Can it write a
woman into existence? Can it help a woman to exist in a world that denies
her complexity? Kimberly Reyes's collection, *Running to Stand Still*, has
made me a believer. Her poems, sonically sharp and mysterious, create a
self that is able to stand, to withstand, the horrors of the past and present.

BRANDI GEORGE, AUTHOR OF *GOG*

What is a "black" woman's body in relation to a woman's body? Everything
except a woman's body, writes Kimberly Reyes. Pinballing between
family lore, social media, and pop culture discourse, Reyes deconstructs
the casual discourses of contempt her narrators are invited to embrace
outside and within blood lines, however much "birthright belonging/
is the maim." And yet, betrayed by the human desire to belong ("To be
kept is to/ be kept, and what you wanted"), they—she—never quite reach
escape velocity: *Running to Stand Still* is thus the poignant record of an
orbit, both victory and impasse.

TYRONE WILLIAMS, AUTHOR OF *AS iZ*

In *Running to Stand Still* Kimberly Reyes excavates the many forces that shape(d) her speaker's black girl-to-womanhood. Several decades of pop lyrics bookend sections of vivid poems that combine matrilineal history with fully self-aware, contemporary survivalism. This is the story of a daughter of 1990s NYC, complete with "teeth-mashing / sweet and sour scenes." Reyes's poems delve into the messy realities of "a / slinking / two-headed / freedom / bare-knuckling / wear and track." Don't be fooled by her assertion that "my narration is jerky, / preemptive, unreliable"—this is about as straight-talking a collection as you're likely to read this year.

IRÈNE MATHIEU, MD, AUTHOR OF OROGENY AND GRAND MARRONAGE

"You signal with the hand you hold.
          The baggage you can / can't manage.

     Makes   them more comfortable around   you."
             you   them

In this bifurcation of *you* and *them*, the reader plays an active role. While reading Kimberly Reyes's profoundly affecting words, I saw myself as the *you* of this moment, of this book. I am compelled to help in carrying the baggage, this weight. I am grateful for having had the experience of moving through this labyrinth of consciousness. This is the important and necessary work of *Running To Stand Still*.

TRUONG TRAN, CO-AUTHOR WITH DAMON POTTER OF 100 WORDS

RUNNING TO STAND STILL

RUNNING TO STAND STILL

KIMBERLY REYES

OMNIDAWN PUBLISHING
OAKLAND, CALIFORNIA
2019

Cover art: Dominique Santos, "We're All Going to Burn
in the Eyes of Happiness"
Website: http://dxminiq.com

Cover typeface: Warnock Pro
Interior typefaces: Minion Pro

Cover & interior design by Cassandra Smith

Printed in the United States
by Books International, Dulles, Virginia
On 55# Glatfelter B19 Antique
Acid Free Archival Quality Recycled Paper

Library of Congress Cataloging-in-Publication Data

Names: Reyes, Kimberly, 1977- author.
Title: Running to stand still / Kimberly Reyes.
Description: Oakland, California : Omnidawn Publishing, 2019.
Identifiers: LCCN 2019017405 | ISBN 9781632430724 (paperback)
Subjects: | BISAC: POETRY / General. | POETRY / American /
    African American.
Classification: LCC PS3618.E9386 A6 2019 | DDC 811/.6--dc23
LC record available at https://lccn.loc.gov/2019017405

Published by Omnidawn Publishing, Oakland, California
www.omnidawn.com (510) 237-5472 (800) 792-4957
10 9 8 7 6 5 4 3 2 1
ISBN: 978-1-63243-072-4

FOR PANSY BROWN

Contents

...you're wholly occupied by pastimes of invisibility.

—Reginald Shephard,
"Johnny Minotaur"

You don't see me but you will
I am not invisible, I am here.

—U2,
"Invisible"

Welcome to your life,
There's no turning back.

—Tears for Fears,
"Everybody Wants to Rule the World"

i.

I hear voices
Leading me on
Urging me on

—Split Enz,
"Voices"

THE BLUEPRINT

I sit with Gwendolyn
we shuck green peas
over large rusty cylinders
over bent ashy knees.
Deep in red clay
she smacks my hand:
Stop fidgeting child
focus.

She says the names don't matter
the tastes, the plains
the lessons are the same
distraction spends time
costs lives:
Fill the bucket.

Snap and stop for the sap of green —
snap and feel the round
the rise under forefinger
snap without stopping.
Snap, stop looking down!
Peas aren't all seeds
let the red ground eat.

The Message

I met Jenifer in our third-grade classroom.

One "n." No time for repetition.

She had advanced leukemia.

That meant *in the bones.*

And he held my hand as our parents whispered.
The "C" word. Her older brother. Chris.

I didn't know any teenage boys who weren't my cousins.
He didn't look like any of them.

He flashed like Saturday morning cartoons.
Eyes sharp and calm. Refractive,
as the Silver Surfer's board.

And my heart beat quick, bushy vibrations on their parents'
brown velvet couch. Beside him. My tongue hung heavy
and loose
            inside a mouth I kept trying to shut. Moist and
shifty palms collapsed, as he slid three fingers into the wet
heat of my hand.

Did I look like a girl?
There, on the couch.

All my friends were boys.
We never talked about it.

The exchange: silver and blue.
Jenifer's big, grainy eyes, wilting
on me, under thinning blond hair.

Knowing what started on that couch,
in that orange living room.

Who I'd become
with slick palms.

Who I'd remain for all her lost seasons.

A fractured
transfixing calm,
a whisper to wait:

(The setting sun, always warmer than its rising.)

Behind the unblemished and blithe.
A long while before I could hold a hand
and look up.

REMEMORY

An August day, the kind when the exhausted concrete hisses
excrement, a lady made my grandmother hand-wash her
underwear. She'd had an accident, this lady, but shame wasn't
her worry. The browned, red chunks of blood
refuse to be combed by her girl Pansy's hands.
Washing machine, too delicate.

Silting only the brown, knotted knuckles
that kneaded another family's sore feet,
caressed their childrens cold, plum cheeks
could meet.

My mother, the one to recall
this day, for me—caution, tribute,
after a two-bus, crosstown commute,
over the scalp of a New York summer.

My grandmother was a domestic.
A home aide. A maid.

My mother's prized appliance:
Her washing machine.
She refines,
near-empty loads,
every night.

Epigenetics, Elegy and Effigy

I found her name
online

Lennison

                my great, great on pixeled
                frayed brown certification
                she was born before the war
                we certainly didn't win and
                though the website wouldn't
                name it,
                born belonging
                to Messrs, Sir
                names that don't matter just
                that they took and
                gave her hers
                forced red South Carolina
                quicksand clay
                under chattel nails.

                No lift
                in that lifetime.

But she planted
grit
that quietly crept
        high enough above the trees
                to name her baby's
        babies. Force their leaves.

I mouth her name
        Lennison
                with every rise

        I belong to her
choreography,

her suffocating whys

her leaping over lives

like my grandmother's
fastening from new man
to new child
to new man
to get a share
cropped her roots

    her six-foot frame

             Lennison flicks my wrist
                 to leap
                       ashen skin
                             the bodiless hands
                                 wooden third
                               eyes

                           drop me in half stride

                             anointing a
                             slinking
                        two-headed
                freedom
            bare-knuckling
       wear and track

the familial   whip   echoing
snake's hiss: freefall   a prodding
crack.

The trapped
girls without proper provenance
women without a world

        that won't claim

us

or how our mothers
only knew
birthright belonging
is the maim

guideless steps
become bloodthirst
we're game.

IMPRINT

In the photo on my fridge my grandmother is wearing a
linen blazer that engulfs her shoulders. As if a man's,
and not just a size too big. As if not made for her
at all. Her white-rimmed glasses have the same
indifference for her body, pinching the bridge of her nose.
Her hair is slicked and pinned in the toil of an
at-least-two-hours-to-wash-press-and-curl bun.
The way her white shirt clings to her clavicle, I can only
imagine the picture was taken on a hot Harlem day.
Maybe August.

I keep it next to the 2009 inauguration photo. Michelle in
felted gold lace.

My grandmother's photograph, crystalline amber,
a Kodak filter she probably paid more for at the local
Woolworths down South. Or Up North. I'm sure she
thought it would make her look sophisticated.

I crack yolks to the steam
hair sizzling inside each tooth
hot comb fighting tired, steady
hands, instance, humidity.
Everything in place,
the next hour or so.
Long enough to
take the picture.

ii.

To the gypsy
That remains
Her face says freedom
With a little fear

—*Fleetwood Mac,*
"Gypsy"

Winter, Cape Town

I have some black family,
he says.
Dreadlock brushing his
crayon-colored-nude shoulder
betrays his
                elevated
subtracted standing.

His girlfriend: Straight hair,
speaks Afrikaans,
slips that she's better than

Africans. *Better educated.*
She's a proper Colored girl.
She corroborates his space.

I no longer know mine
in the cradle of civilization.

Here, I thought we were all Cosby kids.

Air, hemispheres change,
calibrate. I come home to:

Zoe playing Nina,
Lolo mocking Rachel,
Madea she says.
Medea answers.

Remembering my mother's memory:
Ali and Frazier.
A god holding court, in ape face,
and our promise of the golden fleece.

THE WEIGH IN

... a "given" of my existence

as the intolerable
fact that I am dark-complexioned; big-boned;
and once weighed
one hundred and sixty-five pounds ...

— But then I think, No. That's too simple, —

without a body, who can
know himself at all?
Only by
acting; choosing; rejecting; have I
made myself —

Brooklyn, New York. Winter, 2009. (170 pounds): Jordan,
Lebanese and White American, wears disdain for convention,
courtship. On his nape, snaking up his face: A clear python
swallowing a black teardrop. Inked in prison. He can only
meet at night. On sticky Lower East Side bar stools. Under
his stubble. His unwashed sheets. Bad boy fantasy. Boston
Southie. All Adam's apple, he coos: *I beat off thinking about you*
yesterday. I even told my boys about your body. (Wow!) You're
flattered. Flabbergasted.

New London, Connecticut. Spring, 2010. (-32): Chris,
White American, pulls out chairs, opens doors. Tall. Finally
makes you feel like a woman, a girl. Especially when he bends
down. Shouts at you. At home. Outside cafes. (Outside—with
you!) He picks up the tab. Holds your hand. Admires how
even your wrists are tiny. He talks of exes. Constantly. You
meet one. Exotic (and pretty, she was pretty, right? You hope
pretty is his type), petite, Puerto Rican and Chinese. But she

gained weight. His disapproval. His head shake. He finds you between leap years. He loves that you're *not the type to let yourself go.*

Cape Coast, Ghana. Summer, 2012. (+7): Mani, Black Ghanaian, stares from afar. Even still, up close. Up all night, he's high on his *Obruni* prize. The *white black girl.* He's a decade younger, wading in the ancient confidence of the undrowned. The rested. All pluck. Teeth and buoyancy. *Everything here is a fight. Everyone here wants the best.* He enters the ring. Wants one on your finger before you leave. The newness of your curl and tan lines. But he's familiar with your *African shape.* Owns it some nights. Thinks that you'll see him as more than a summer. Forgets you're still playing to win.

Harlem, New York. Fall, 2012. (+5): Michael, Black American, talks over you in African-American studies. Fixes his glare after class. *A drink, perhaps?* Still, you're the *clueless voice of the middle class.* He asks you for singles to tip the bathroom attendant. He's teaching. He's light-skinned. You call him mini-Barack. But he's louder. Down-er. Explains his role in the struggle: *Dating girls browner than he desires. Browner, even, than you* to suppress his white supremacist thoughts. (This is a compliment? Yes!) This is the compliment you take.

Cape Town, South Africa. Winter, 2013. (Holding): Rudy, Colored South African, reminds: *You're not mixed, like us.* Coiled blonde dreadlock brushing his chubby arm. He's right. Righteous. The ocean never obscured his view. He shows you dusty townships. Shaded cafes of the DNC rich. You run into his old classmate at the mall. Her name he can't recall. *He used to play with Black girls. Just not an African-American.* (Perform Michelle. An opening. A way in.) His Colored girlfriend shows up at happy hour. Small, curly, curvy and caramel. It's hours before he introduces you. You appreciate everything the hyphen can erase.

Chicago, Illinois. Summer, 2013. (Not Counting): Romeo, White Italian, covers your escaping thoughts with toothy kisses. Broken-English babble of *Cappuccino babies*. Language is not the barrier. He texts pictures of pink roses and his penis. He's short. You rebuff invitations to The Navy Pier. Going out. Playing house. One glass. You're halfway through, wine, before the doorbell rings. Fermenting saliva. Salt. Rubber and worry: His expiring visa. A last chance. He strokes your skin, searches for fluency, *just like Serena Williams.*

> — *How her soul, uncompromising,*
> *insatiable,*
> > *Must have loved eating the flesh from her bones,*
>
> *revealing this extraordinarily*
> *mercurial; fragile; masterly creature …*
>
> — *Frank Bidart,*
> *"Ellen West"*

Timed Out of New York

Ordering off the off
menu at Veselka.
2am army of sloshed
sauerkraut-eating
blintz besties, flashing
out-of-town, post-
Palladium kids the real
music of the city
through teeth-mashing
sweet and sour scenes:

Bartering for space,
freestyle mixtapes on
Bleeker,
(buying from Papito,
who knew Lisa Lisa,
before)
the after-school run to 8th
in black Lycra for nubuck
buttered Doc Martens.

Tapping chicken's feet on
Canal,
between the grey third
rail and a magic yellow
Sports Walkman's
stomping bass.

Mouth breathing through
the smack of expired
Chinatown. August.
Know better than sandals
antagonizing rats with red
toes on snarled subway
platforms.

A warring chorus of singing
street poets, not soliciting
vegetables: *'Shroom haven,*
get a piece of heaven,
hustling
marked time on St. Marks.

Gleaning from glistening
Drag Queens, at Mac,
on Christopher.
Gentle, patient, painted,
nodding, dirty-platinum men.
The first to stare: *You're*
beautiful, to the drum of
the Jungle Brothers.

Underage and
overstimulated
ambition gnarled
with the Blonde's.
We blinked.

Black and Brown
vogue snatched. Up
town, 3am 4 train.

You're in a position
    You had no choice in the
        Voices
            You are reappropriating
                Did you know?

iii.

Smile
like you mean it

—The Killers,
"Smile Like You Mean It"

Opening Lines

You keep asking where I'm from.
I've said NYC twice, twice.
Second generation.

You keep examining like,
there's no equation
like we somehow began at the sum.

Like later, you won't try to impress
with a Wu-Tang lyric,
liberties with a Chappelle set.

Like you don't know where we are
what we've built.

Like you don't know me.

You keep asking where we're from.

Because the hyphen
sits, no direction

like we're still

in   between.

You keep the game going
with interrogation.

You keep
repeating
the question.

THE UNCANNY VALLEY

After Kara Walker's "A Subtlety" at the Domino Sugar Factory
Brooklyn, 2014

They came in between me and the Sugar Baby.
A marvel. Inside a moment of prayer.

Flick of blonde hair. Phone in my face: *Take our photo?!*

> *"Repeat Repeat Repeat"*
> *— Kara Walker, Do You Like Crème*
> *in Your Coffee and Chocolate in Your Milk?*

Right here. Still wet air.
No space.
Smiles and crass. Snaps of our nipples.
Our ass.
Your mammy.
Our matriarch.

This is hip. This is art.
This is it

molasses. Blanched white.

You won't?!
God,
you girls, like, always need a fight!

> *"... the romance of it,*
> *the storytelling—it was so rich*
> *and epic, and that was what I hadn't*
> *expected. I hadn't expected to be titillated*
> *in the way that stories like that are meant to*
> *titillate. And, at the same time, it was so much*
> *fodder for the work that I wanted to do."*
> *— Kara Walker,*
> *on exploiting the exploitation in Gone With the Wind*

This is church. This is collateral. This is holy terrain.
I am ekphrasis, imbued to the frame.

WHAC-A-MOLE

After See Through
by Njideka Akunyili Crosby

The queen. Your queen to be.

Queen Bee. Be:

Formica and wall paper.

Beige and benign.

Be behind glass.

Be front line.

Be bold.

Be coaled canary.

Be cloaked.

Be coated.

Be afloat.

Be drowning.

Be drowned out.

When they've had you before they've met you / it's difficult to decide on which terms they can have you and look pretty   when you smile.

iv.

Skating around the truth of who I am
But I know that, the ice is getting thin

—Tori Amos,
"Winter"

BELOVED
After Toni Morrison

More than Pop Tarts,
Bruce Banner,
my mom's quick wit
our shared triumph,
her beam, still fighting,
still light in *irises*
the color of her skin.

Hearing her ignite
through the voice
of her dog,
her delight in playing
ventriloquist
for the sponge
weathering the waves
of the strange hide and meet
he obediently observed

her banter, her barking,
lulled us.

More than the smell of blood,
peroxide,
falling off my dusty pink
Mrs. Pac Man skateboard,
the scent of soreness from
our laughter:
my grounding.

I didn't know how much the scars would count.

How age would become collage
without the speckled blood pavement
I could scrape the white
off my fingernails
connect the dots on.

How I'd mourn the dog
she had to forget she buried
because it was an accident
because of her baby brother
who fought
the hallucinations,
scarlet scenes,
a beloved,
too tuned to this world
sans small peach pills.

The interruption, quick:

A paw wound for tending,
small licks needing
cleansing.
A stove pot, toppled over.
A house left to
bare bone.

The exit, simple:

Two wood boxes, under red clay,
caked cryonic fear
when she buried her mother,
the coming year.

The smell of boiled fur
hanging,

I still remember

the most innocent suffering
the most cruelty.

I learned.
She prayed.

For her, the specifics
melted away,

hid in the merciful wings of
dismemory

panning out
painting a sigh, tethering a glance,
she used to be able to do that,
but survival required broad strokes
with the new *slits of irons*
framing her nose
balancing the weight

my compass
struggling to
see straight.

A piece of him

                                  And one afternoon,

the red star
suspended on a pierced
Kelly green cap, a starfish
caught in cryosleep,

fell out of my brown lunch bag,
in a crop of crinkled brown lunch bags,
slinky hunched, on the
Senior Lunch Bench:

Turkey, tomatoes, capers, cheese
prudence, post-its, grooming,
arugula, tuna, white bread, rye.

                                  Our home, opened

to the clank of steel on asphalt
                iron to echo
                unraveling
that day
that Heineken top

                                  dropped out.

low self esteem is an addiction
like any other

FUNCTIONING

A ziplocked lunch, recycled bag:
Rye and overripe tomatoes.

Red-eyed up and early
respite from regret wrapped

as aspiration. Unfinished
exposed hems.

MARKED

"... an overgrowth of the cells that create pigment (color) in
skin ..."
—kidshealth.org

A mole or beauty mark. A curse or birthmark. Or
meets in between,　　　mine, on the upper left
bridge of my nose. My brother, mother have the
Cindy Crawford-mole we all wanted,
　　　　　except Cindy, before the world
approved her mutation.

"There are no desires, shameful or innocent, that one's
progeny does not publicly disclose."
—Marie-Hélène Huet
Monstrous Imagination

All my grandparents had moles. My mother said
it's a Caribbean thing. All my grandparents are
from the Caribbean.　　　Except my
mother's mother.

"... birthmarks were the result of the mother's unfulfilled
desires."
—Marie-Hélène Huet paraphrasing Lorenz Heister in
Monstrous Imagination

My mom would visualize dimples, large doe eyes, like my
cousins　　　on my father's side: Slick jetting black
hair, caramel skin
I just wanted the mole. Then.

"... found at birth (congenital) or developing later in life
(acquired) ..."
—encyclopedia.com

My birthmark appeared in 4th grade. I wasn't
born with it.
        Which already makes me a liar.
The mark is not by birth.

The mark doesn't appear in baby pictures.
I can't be expected to recollect every detail.

REYES

On still Saturdays, I'd disappear
into a plush brown
love seat in father's mother's faded beige
living room. We'd watch white
dead-eyed slashers
expose eager, glistening bodies,
Jason, Freddy, and Michael —
masked stowaways
(I understood to be)
birthed beneath the red Atlantic,
explaining gore and the many doors of
no return to a child, prying
for a way back home.

We were one
we were Mestizo Red,
my yellow grandmother and me.
The machete sugarcane bled
Red on the island
dark and Jíbaro, Salinas poor,
Red was the language we spoke,
fertile in storied humility.
The good Red on the Mainland,
the mixed and other and ancient and othered,
rich *got some Indian in me* reigning Red

whose scorn I

I didn't know then.

The

why is your last name Reyes, is your husband Spanish?

this.

Then, we had only the scripted anodyne
Red leaking out of the screen.

HER, MAYBE

I wore the face of a Mestizo
dream, evening before last.

She looked a little more,
maybe. In between,
my parents.

So less pronounced
and plainly,
regal.

Last name
easier to spout.

Our face
recognized
all their mouths.

v.

The silly champion
She says she can't go home
Without a chaperone

—Elvis Costello,
"Accidents Will Happen"

Heavy

Nerves and beige chunks
Kentucky Fried Chicken
from the top bunk
you released dinner.

Your mom, the best cook in the neighborhood
(the only cook in the neighborhood)
of gossiping, working moms.

Your father was bringing
dinner home. Slaw, tension
biscuits, regret
the other room,
the secret recipe.

Your mom warned, *lower your voice*
she's already having a hard time at school.

The next day was school

Journal entry May 2, 1987:

"Things would be easier if I looked like Maria.
Bet it doesn't take so long to wash her hair."

"GROSS, I CAN'T PUT MY HANDS IN YOUR HAIR
WITHOUT GETTING THEM GETTING GREASY?!"

Every morning, before the warming

Cream of Wheat,

a wide mane brush,

bristling struggle

stretched and partitioned my roots.

Unnatural labor, made easier over

a cool pink pomade sold to black

mothers praying to the confident, polished

brown baby girls with

perky pigtails coating its round

plastic containers.

Once my shiny head left my

mother's hopeful hands

I'd let it drop, gyrate, shake to

hear the clanging lilac barrettes

boasting hard-earned coils,

twisted in time and affection.

My mother wanted me to shine;

my pastels and pomp

swayed to clink in unison.

Eric was the approval

every girl wanted.

Every day he picked me

first, for his manhunt team.

Salt, prudence dripped

from my head as we raced

around the fenced-in asphalt,

faster than the other

girls, not afraid of contact.

Confrontation: the only way

to tag, to win. We always did.

On the last day of fourth grade

I held down a weaker girl,

her face coated in conditional

retreat and matted blonde wisps.

Eric pet my head in approval,

slowly lifted his fingers,

changed his mind.

THE DISAPPEARED

I lost a 66-pound Black girl.
They're left all the time.

She wasn't misplaced:
neglected—indulged
then detested.

No social media whistles,
she vanished:
Weight Watchers key,
new wardrobe.

I was sick of hiding
she was sick of fighting,
sharing house with spite.

"Jane Cookie Doe," maybe,
a stretch-marked
unmanned grave
swallowing

a steely frame,
a Tribute:
suffocated nights,
barren inertia.

But without ceremony
her phantom limbs ignite.
Starved from sin,
inflate

back to life

flaccid flesh
in wake
building armor.

But I count and remember.
Count, run her down.

Count and run her
back into the ground.

WANT. MY MTV.

More than AIDS, Arthur Ashe said
his true burden was being Black.
C.C. DeVille said being a junkie
was sexier than being fat.

Everything I know I learned from TV.

So my narration is jerky,
preemptive, unreliable.

I know Madonna said power
is being told you're not loved
undesirable
and not being destroyed

between commercial breaks.

UPON INQUIRING

why I got
my invite
so late
Eve informed me
of the 2nd bat mitzvah list.
Praise be the lords
who parcel the rule book.
I loved her,
I love her—
went anyway.

vi.

Don't believe in yourself
Don't deceive with belief

—David Bowie,
"Quicksand"

Push Notifications

I haven't slept well
Since

It can't be counted   In
linear
Not a measure
More a mark
    Or rewinding

  This part

These restless

   lips   S
     Fated
     Fluidity
     Into
Concrete times

    To disembody

Anticipation

Even
in the moment

like static
like worry
like doubt
like masturbation
wine on the couch

feels like film and plastic
feels like reel and repetition

feels behind glass
feels already distant
you're watching

       when it arrives

checking your reflection in his eyes.

2.14

9:33am

A spot! You're 12 minutes earlier than your 15-minute-early goal. You found a spot. You're already making it work, today.

9:33:30am

The spot's by a fast food drive-in. It's a real spot, but you see why it's open. A little too close to the driveway. Getting sideswiped, a nightmare you can't add. Smart people pass this up. They don't take the bad spots. They have the confidence to stroll in a few minutes late. There's enough time to find another spot.

9:34am

Pace up and down and around the decision. Wince when cars get too close. You should move. You should move the car for peace of mind. It's not too late. Move the car. You're supposed to be meditating on faith. You found this spot.

9:35am

It's too late to move the car. You have an appointment. You can't make them wait.

9:38am

Leave car.

9:42am

Two-step turn. Check the bumper one more time. Clench your stomach and turn towards the Drug and Alcohol Intake on Fillmore. Walk. Cross. Take note of how much you don't like this street, can't come back.

9:44am

Open the clinic door with your sleeve. This is the responsible thing to do. Catch things before they spiral. You're good at this. Catching. Measuring. The damage already accumulated. Both your therapists agree. It's (probably) situational. But in case.

9:45am

Fold into the instant stick of hot, candy breath and sanitizer. Dirty, eggshell-tiled floors. Fidgeting hands and elevated, tone-deaf greetings exchanged mid-conversation. Disquiet. You were too honest. You're always too honest, too late. That's why you're here. No one checks the correct boxes on health-intake forms. It should have gone, a routine physical.

9:55am

The first counselor wishes you a happy Valentine's Day. You have to recall the last 30 days, how many without a drink? It's been almost a year. Today, also Fat Tuesday. There are ways to count, ounces in drinks. Binging denies a cruel imperial chart. *Were you abused?* Always the oddest query. Do you know what that means? Perspective makes it an impossible question. Recalibration says, don't be dramatic.

10:13am

You're led with a plastic urine cup. Told to leave your purse on the chair, the nurse will watch. The bathroom has no sink. You can't be trusted with water. No mirror. You can't be. No one here is allowed to see their fingerprint. It's feigned sanitization. It's a false profile you surrender. It's only that piece of you.

10:19am

Drained. You step outside and ask where you can wash your hands. There's a sink in the hallway. You wash in front of the half-sleeping man you saw earlier. He's slinky hunched in a chair and indifferent to your ceremony. His heart rate is seductive. You mime his breaths. Every 11 seconds. You haven't slept in days. You're asked if it's ok to be weighed. You say, no. It's only blood you're offering.

SCAR CITY

The need to keep
a wineglass half full

is not optimism.

It's holy
want,

wood-laminate
kneeling,

preemptive and recessive

promises, half
winces and

ashy nights,
knee-

deep
in stigmata.

In the weeds

Decades
I wish I'd slept through entirely

bowed black
dahlia in lily
fields, all
white noise
and patience
asked,
a bode:

bloom days
to pull out, play,
at best
honey-lacquered hours

I slept through entirely.

Researching white outs, erasure, and sonnets at the library, on a Friday night

They can't see the equation without you
at the bottom

You can't see the equation ~~without~~
you at the bottom

You can't see the equation

It's zero-sum

The mental and physical harm

you offer yourself to prove ~~them wrong~~

you offer yourself to prove them wrong

you offer yourself ~~to prove them wrong~~

Proximity

You signal with the hand you hold.
          The baggage you can / can't manage.

Makes   them more comfortable around   you.
     you   them

Prescriptive Fires

Late-night lyrics in the Lyft:

All my bitches got their real hair.

Chris Brown needs us to know.
He's winning.
He's gonna *hit it*.
It hits you.

You've never been a perfect victim
or a perfect bitch.

Only the parchest tinder.

vii.

Bring back that child she said
Spare me the price of freedom

—*Duran Duran,*
"Proposition"

Hey beautiful

I love your hair

And smile

You are a writer. It made me smile. Very descriptive.

I swiped right because I love your hair and great smile. Great face really. That's all I know this far 😊

I love that beautiful hair of yours...

Do you feel SF is too white?

Don't worry, I'm white on the outside and black on the inside.

You seem like uncomplicated and warm person. Would you like to meet up sometime? I am curious where is the catch ;-)

Best,

This is definitely what I do. I always message the pretty ones first. If none agrees to come over (quite rare), I go for the fatter ones. Those are the last resorts/slumpbusters, particularly if I haven't fulfilled my quota yet.

Not only do I prioritize girls by net weight, I also prioritize by race, in this order:

-Skinny white
-Skinny Asian
-Skinny Latina/black
-Fat white
-Fat Asian
-Fat Latina

I don't do fat black... That's really dredging the bottom of the barrel. And I mean fat, not obese. A little chub here and there, nothing crazy. Definitely nothing above 200 lbs.

16 hours ago · Like · Reply · 5

1.3K   910 Comments   104 Shares

you are enchanting and so sexy, I want to cuddle you and adore you and own you and make you feel desired for longterm, do you dislike it?

viii.

I never said I was tough
That was everyone else
So you're a fool to attack me
For the image that you built yourself

Just sounds more vicious
Than I actually mean
I really am soft
Yes, I'm tender and sweet

—Sinéad O'Connor,
"You Cause as Much Sorrow"

AFTER HIM

who claims you

who all, together

don't disappoint
so differently
than the apparition who raised you

worried what people
wonder

worry

People may look at us
funny, won't know
we're related

rendering
inferred distress

to a shame

impossible to understand

watching a chiseled father, lithe
blonde daughter on the F train

a cradle, a firm hold, a
tunneled view of
paternal pride

and when you're most jealous
voyeuring girlishness, guiltlessness

you watch father and son films, too
The Red Balloon, Road to Perdition
where the tarnish resolves the bond

you always knew who your person was
always a picture of belonging,
but could only grasp

this new man's
materialized hand

The thing you love

about dating sociopaths:
You get to be profiled
You get to be front
Center
Prey

Hot Headlights

you get to be doe,
bright eyed, small,
in someone's sight

ix.

And is evil just something you are,
or something you do

—Morrissey,
"Sister I'm a Poet"

The Body

you keep reading about this woman
you don't know
(Maybe you knew?)
back in j-school,
it was j-school so,
really,
details you should remember.
this woman disappeared.

people (Some you know you know.)
are memorializing
and celebrating her work.
they say she was smart, fearless,
always smiling.

divers found her head
today,

                and suddenly you realize
            you didn't know it was missing,
         you didn't know what happened,
                  you scrolled but,

stopped to read a funny post
about Project Runway.
thought about Heidi Klum
how her nickname was "the body."
(You always thought that was weird
Heidi Klum sold makeup, too,
which required a face,
or at the very least,
a smile
to attach to
the body.)

(Tim Gunn is your hero.)

the name of the woman you (don't) know is Kim,
was Kim,
you should have remembered another Kim
in your cohort, but she's not familiar.

not even when you see
her headshot
in the email
for the memorial at your school. (There have been a few.)

she was maybe your age,
but strawberry blonde,
and when she took the photo,

maybe there was a fan
in the room (?)
or she'd just turned her head
for the flash
at exactly the right time,
which is hard to do
'cause she was engulfed,
strands of orbiting
amber flames
crystallized, aglow.

(You remember Madonna's
hair floated the same way in
the "Live to Tell" video.)

(There was a Project Runway contestant
Stella, who'd pronounce "leather"
without the "r,"
which you didn't pick up at first
'cause you're from New York,
but then you saw
how it was funny
how it became a joke

how people can be funny
without even trying
if being funny just means
people are laughing at you.)

(You'd watch Project Runway in bed
with this man
with blue and red snake tattoos,
who also secretly loved Tim Gunn
and Stella.
he had a thick Boston accent that tickled
as you'd both slowly coo "leatha"
back at the screen.

once,
through vodka breath
he told you the only reason
you were in his bed:
your body

he could take
or leave
your smile.)

(Snakeskin is leather,
turns out
turning out cattle
isn't the only way,
could be any hide.
snakeskin can be expensive,
tends to cost more
when there's an ornamental
head
attached to the skin
of what used to be
a complete body.)

it took probably a month, or
more than months
from what you could tell

from what people
you vaguely knew
were saying,
curated clicks
(Round, yellow faces,
a single tear.)
more than a month
to figure out
if it was an accident.

you were just skimming
supposed
maybe she fell off the boat (?)
for a while, you thought
it could have been negligence
she could have been drinking
partying, smiling on this boat
when something bad happened.
(No one's fault.)

                            ("Make it Work!"
                    is what Tim Gunn would snap
                                at contestants
                        and why he's your hero.)

            (At least some of us try.)

turns out Kim was
reporting
about a man
on his boat,
the way you learned in j-school:
studying a man
in his natural habitat.

one of the news stories
you finally ingested
said this man had fantasies
about women's heads
mutilated torsos,
burnt bodies.

Kim was probably killed by this man.
this man she probably didn't know
before she got on his submarine.
(A sub,
not the dreamboat you'd envisioned.)

>and you know
>you don't know what happened,
>you scrolled but—
>didn't know the story at all.

@ Planned Parenthood the Week Before the Inauguration

...grace could not come to the wolf from its own despair, only
through some external mediator, so that, sometimes, the beast
will look as if he half welcomes the knife that despatches him.
—Angela Carter
"The Company of Wolves"

Plotting an Instagramable picture, dodging Cabinet
and dick pics, you're going on another date with
Greg, a Slovenian from Hungary who *first touched*
himself when Black girls like you were still a tube
and glass plate away,

                              bouncing balls
on clay courts.

He's not your type. Bald, but, baiting. His *ex-*
girlfriend is Kenyan so he pries, kneads his
fingers through your hair to ensure *all that curl*, the
virtue, really grows *there*, because he needs you to
know he *knows* about *these things*.

(Like the stranger two strangers ago who asked if your
father was a light-skinned Puerto Rican,
which could explain why you're *so pretty*, he
grew up in a Black neighborhood and also *knows*.)

Greg says you *think in binaries*. As he kisses he
rubs his ring finger over your brows and collapsed
boundaries to see how easily they'll smudge. *It's*
too much. Thumb presses the pimple on your chin.
So you're not perfect, after all. What? What's wrong?
I'm telling you I think you're perfect. You don't need so
much makeup.

(The new president doesn't open the car door
or hold the First Lady's hand. Even progressives
feel badly for Melania. The familiar. The victim.
You remember Melania is a birther.)

Cruelty is his sophistication and he *has his needs*
and *needs the beauty* he kneads your *flat stomach, so
beautiful,* as he grabs the fat of your upper thigh

...you can lose this quickly, you know. He grabs and
grabs your hand and you keep going, daring and
bargaining and begging for grace, trapped in all the
muck and fluidity of the in-between space.

> (Zsa Zsa Gabor died the day you met
> Greg. Nine marriages in nearly 100 years
> of performance. And *Greg* isn't his real
> name, he eventually confesses.)

And it's your life exposed.

He was bored at home, in a rut, and his *girlfriend,*
who maybe knows, but would *probably only mind if
he was sloppy,* is back home *in a hut* and, *man,* now
he *feels bad.*

You *should know,* although this was play, you're
an *upgrade.* She's *an unsophisticated girl, you're from
New York, you're fancy.* Can he *stay*?

> (They're from The City. Your city:
> Civilization. This new president, your
> old mayor tell a joke about a firefighter
> getting *lucky* after 9/11. At the
> Inauguration lunch. You can't keep
> yours down. You need the papers.
> Confirmation. The nurse understands.)

To let that fall asleep next to you, inside of you, what
does the touch of it do? Truth is you don't believe in
it, you constantly dare it, or are it, if it exists. Truth
is, liars are the most reliable people you know

write about this, he says.

IT FELT LIKE LOVE.

"You won. He wants you… Do you know how many women would give their left leg to have a man… publicly claim them? It's not like you're some skank that he blew out, who's got to resort to taking secret selfies with the man while he sleeps. You're his lady."
— *Mary Jane Paul*
"Getting Serious"
Being Mary Jane, BET

> Legacy
> Love
> Attached
> Cold
> Tongue
> Hold

"But it felt like love to me. It embraced me. I accepted it and thought, 'Well, this is how he loves.' I got that from my mother and from my grandmother, who were abused."
— *Michel'le on her relationship with Dr. Dre,*
Elle Magazine

> Lashing
> Lasting
> Care
> Calm
> Claim
> Owning
>
> Ownership
> Owning
> Owners
> Beauty
> Pride
> Tribe

*"Getting beat was love to me. When I got with Suge,
believe it or not, he didn't really beat me. I asked him 'why aren't
you beating me? Don't you love me?'"*

*— Michel'le on her relationship with Suge Knight,
R&B Divas LA reunion, TV One*

Hold
Still
Safety
Froze

Hold
Still

Choosing
Chosen
Owning
Claiming
Owning
Owned

Building
Status
Home

Heat Lightning/The Split Tree

Don't stand so close to the window
Somebody out there might see
And you're not supposed to be here with me
The walls have ears and the darkness has eyes
don't you see?

—Paul Kelly and the Stormwater Boys,
"Don't Stand So Close to the Window"

My grandmother's body was still, with us
weeks after she tried to leave, weeks after

my mother, always nervous,
thunderstorms, begged me

away from the window, flashing
jewelry, three clanking bangles,

superstition
says: Don't tempt a roused fate

my grandmother brought back
from a trip to the Bahamas, her dream week

her second time on a plane
at sixty-three, solo

still working, still bold enough to
save, fly, buy silver.

My grandmother's first time on a plane:
Taking me down to South Carolina

to see the farm
the fabled nothing that kept her

from becoming something, kept giving
her babies—*just one look*, she'd *swell*

she forewarned: The consequence of sass.
And heat. And one day, the opening came

to leave the weeds and beatings, a
chance Up North, for cleaning house.

I shook my silver at the   cracking
lavender and pink sky

running on preordained rage and
showing my ass and

asking for trouble,   beckoning
prepubescent summer rain

in July, New York City
the phone rang: Woodhull hospital.

The weeds came calling.

36 days—no insurance—electrical outages,
backup generators, a coma that also refused

                                        her offering,
                                        mercy—

a stroke the doctors misnamed, respirators
jutting mangles, exploited remains.

She awoke, still, slant,
face—bile—tubes

snaking their way through
her

bidding I pretend to forget

escape,   betrayed her
body

finally left in August

in cascades of acidic sweat.

Housekeeping

*"... her physical self is no longer reviled... she is very welcome
to come to the party; indeed, it's not really a party unless she
does come... But in place of the old disgust comes a new kind of
cannibalism."*
—Zadie Smith
"Getting In and Out
Who owns black pain?"
Harper's Magazine, June 2017

You've been inside,
before, dark basements,
fraternity parties:
The butt and the joke.

High fives, back-turned
mutter:

      Fat Albert.

Dopplered laughter.

  .

  .

  .

He needs to tell you
you need him to tell you
that's no longer

this

whip smart
white, rich
wants you pregnant

make it legit.
Sidestepping his harem, *exotic*
Thai and Chinese women, mixed babies,
his Facebook displays. Conquests,
stripes, feathers to hang, calls you *the new wife.*

He likes *being king.* Likes
bidding the darker, already tendered,
tired of *white breast meat*:
Too tough, rough, by daylight.

Houses and litters: Commitment,
enlist, *before you get too old,*
like the other *birds,* inhabited, turned
cheeks—did and do *as they are told.*

His PhD in mathematics, two-bottles-of-red-in,
Venn diagram of *exes* and all your unique
gifts: *Well read, good body, good in bed...*
only about ten pounds to play with.

But you're in
small company.
Finally
small.

You meet his banker friends he's
told all about the new *trophy*
wife and the dizzying envy-
inducing life, he's offering you

honesty. He'd happily change
your last name once you have some *real skin*
in the game: A mulatto baby, a ring, fanfare, security,
clout. After you prove *you can still pop one out.*

You've kept wait, now you're
Wanted. They kiss foreheads and
cradle your waste. To be kept is to
be kept, and what you wanted:

Limp and framed.

Not too much.
The tightrope
of just enough. Wedged up.

Even foreign men smell candied
trauma. Target legacied shame.
Like a sugary branding
burning scabs of your name.

You've placated / baited
the someones. To get in, you remember
scraping your knees on the windowsill.

Bloodied, but clear. To walk away.

BRONZEVILLE WOMEN

"...that part is not true."

—*Carolyn Bryant Donham*

Gwendolyn woke me up this morning:
Child, stop sulking
the grace you scorn, we've always worn.

See, it was always him,
her
in the Tallahatchie.

I had to tell Carolyn's story
keep pen to pad —
you think we only get *Quatrains*

but what happens to us,
them, the collective stain,

weakens the quilt, fastens chains.

Logistical Notes

The italicized phrases that appear in these poems without quotation marks (that are not parts of epigraphs, broken epigraphs, song lyrics, or movie titles) are direct quotes pulled from the narrator's journey, to the best of her recollection. The first exception is in "The Blueprint" where the italicized words are part of an imagined conversation. The second exception is in "Beloved," where the italics reference words or phrases used in Toni Morrison's novel *Beloved*. The third exception is in "Bronzeville Women," where "Quatrains" is italicized. This is to commemorate the Gwendolyn Brooks poem "The Last Quatrain of the Ballad of Emmett Till."

The images on pages 78-80 are screenshots of select messages the narrator received over the course of a week through online dating sites, and a Facebook discussion on *The Love Life of an Asian Guy's* feed that same week.

Conceptual Notes

This book is a dark 21st-century fairytale set to music, short attention spans, and long memory.

The narration takes place inside a Black female body more attached to outside narratives, lyrics, stories, dreams, dream relationships, and images, than herself.

Once she turns down the noise she discovers boundaries, real and perceived, societal and self-imposed, and the wonderful and horrific things that happen when they are breached.

LITERARY ACKNOWLEDGMENTS

These poems and variations of these poems first appeared in/
on *poets.org*, *The Feminist Wire*, *The Acentos Review*, *RHINO*,
Yemassee, *Obsidian*, *New American Writing*, *Columbia Journal*,
MARY: A Journal of New Writing, *LEVELER*, *Juked*, *Cosmonauts
Avenue*, *SWWIM*, *Moko Magazine*, *Paris Lit Up*, *Belleville Park
Pages*, *Transfer*, *Atrocious Poets' Cut Poems from Air: Gwendolyn
Brooks Tribute* and the *Red Light Lit Poetry Anthology*.

Personal Acknowledgments

Thank you to Georgeann, Alex, and Alex, my hearts and souls. There is no facing this world without you.

As always, thank you to Pansy Brown and Tovelle McKiver.

Rachel Sur, my rose, my guide, my oldest and wisest friend, I love you. I know what that is now. You and Jordan Mintzer will always be my all-horns, Capricorn-Taurus, all-star tribe. I'm so grateful to have met my most favorite friends at my most impressionable. It keeps the bar high and keeps me chasing the junior-high-school-passion dragon.

Alice Quinn, thank you for opening and holding the door. Your friendship and encouragement have meant to world to me.

Rusty Morrison and Omnidawn, thank you for the opportunity. Cassandra Smith thank you for holding my hand and for being the best partner in design.

Truong Tran, thank you for not letting me fade into the background and for being the first person to say, "so when is your fucking book coming out?" before it was anything I could envision.

Camille Dungy and the Napa Valley Writers' Conference, being seen, truly seen (in such a serene place) was a healing and affirming experience. I will work to pay it forward.

Meg Schoerke, thank you for going above and beyond and for being the consummate professional and professor.

Irène Mathieu, thank you for being a hilarious roomie, my first editor inside a tornado, and a trusted literary partner.

Nekesa Moody, Tanner Stransky, Justin Reed, Julie Ulrich, Mike Marlin, Nicholas Lemann and Valerie Wallace, thank you for your recs and generosity, I couldn't have gotten to the next level without them. Valerie, a special thank you for being a great teacher and not telling me I was a terrible poet when I was a terrible, baby poet. Nekesa, I still owe you a kidney for assigning me that Duran Duran interview.

Alanna Rickards-Vaught, thank you for grace and for helping to keep me sane during the writing of this book. That was no small task.

Krisztina Karvovszki, thank you reminding what it means to prioritize someone when you mean to prioritize someone, time-zones and datelines be damned.

Karel Banks, thank you for being the guide and mentor I needed when I needed it most.

Whitney Lynch and Sharon Grossman, thank you for your genuine and timely care.

Thank goodness for WLIR (once 92.7 FM in the NYC area), for music, for movies, for Holly Robinson (Peete), Robin Givens, Kim Fields, Lark Voorhies and the fleeting ability I had to see myself as a very (imagined) ordinary Black woman in the 1980s, on TV.

And to all whose names were changed/rearranged, thank you for your participation. Sometimes the unravelings were beautiful, sometimes the skin was ripped off, sometimes willingly shed. However the circumstance, I'm glad to have left the carcasses there.

Kimberly Reyes is a poet and essayist who has received fellowships from the Poetry Foundation, Columbia University, the Fulbright program, Callaloo and San Francisco State University, among other places. Her nonfiction appears in *The Associated Press, The Atlantic, Entertainment Weekly, Time.com, The New York Post, The Village Voice, Alternative Press, ESPN the Magazine, NY1 News, Jane, Entropy, Medium,* and *The Best American Poetry blog,* among other places. Her poetry appears in/on places like *The Academy of American Poets, The Feminist Wire, The Acentos Review, RHINO, Columbia Journal, Yemassee, Obsidian,* and *Eleven Eleven.* Her nonfiction book of essays *Life During Wartime* won the 2018 Michael Rubin Book Award and her poetry chapbook *Warning Coloration* was released by dancing girl press in 2018.

Running to Stand Still
by Kimberly Reyes

Cover art: Dominique Santos,
"We're All Going to Burn in the Eyes of Happiness"
Website: http://dxminiq.com

Cover typeface: Warnock Pro
Interior typefaces: Minion Pro

Cover & interior design by Cassandra Smith

Printed in the United States
by Books International, Dulles, Virginia
On 55# Glatfelter B19 Antique
Acid Free Archival Quality Recycled Paper

Publication of this book was made possible in part by gifts from
Katherine & John Gravendyk in honor of Hillary Gravendyk,
Francesca Bell, and Mary Mackey,

Omnidawn Publishing
Oakland, California
Staff and Volunteers, Fall 2019

Rusty Morrison & Ken Keegan, senior editors & co-publishers
Kayla Ellenbecker, production editor
Gillian Olivia Blythe Hamel, senior poetry editor & book designer
Trisha Peck, senior poetry editor & book designer
Cassandra Smith, poetry editor & book designer
Sharon Zetter, poetry editor & book designer
Liza Flum, poetry editor
Matthew Bowie, poetry editor
Juliana Paslay, fiction editor
Gail Aronson, fiction editor
Rob Hendricks, *Omniverse* editor & marketing assistant
Clare Sabry, marketing assistant
Lucy Burns, marketing assistant
Hiba Mohammadi, marketing assistant
SD Sumner, copyeditor